HOW TO

PREPARE

FOR YOUR CHILD'S FIRST SKI

LESSON

What Every Parent Should Know when Preparing Your Child's First Ski Lesson

'Animated drawing of a child skiing down the slope'

A Quick Guide for:

- Mentally preparing your child for skiing
- How to prepare your child for the outdoors
- Getting the right equipment
- Preparing for safety
- What to expect from the first lesson?
- How to choose the right coach

Herbert K. Naito

508 West 26th Street KEARNEY, NE 68848
402-819-3224
info@medialiteraryexcellence.com

Something about the Author

He spent 40 years in the medical profession. For fun, he coached skiing for over 20 years. He is a member of the Professional Ski Instructors of America, and is certified in Alpine Skiing, Level 2; Adaptive Specialist Level 1; Children's Specialist, Level 2; PSIA Senior Specialist, Level 2; and Children's Trainer. Currently, he is employed by the Vail Resort and is presently on the Vail Educational Staff. He was the former Director of the Children's Advanced Training Specialist, and the Express Pre- School Ski School Programs.

In addition to this book, he has written seven other books on skiing:

(1) A Comprehensive Guide for Coaching Children How to Ski,

(2) The Funky Donkey Tells His Story About His First Ski Lesson

(3) Coaching Wacky Racoon, Children, and Adults the Fundamentals of Good Sportsmanship,

(4) The Hidden Secrets of Having Fun At and Around the Ski Resorts

(5) How to Create Fun for Children with Disabilities on the Ski Slopes

(6) How to Create Successful Ski Lesson Plans for Senior Citizens

(7) How God Prepared & Inspired Me to be a Writer and Author

TABLE OF CONTENTS

INTRODUCTION

It happened to me. It may have happened to you too; not only once, but twice, or even more. How many times have you gone into the store to purchase a product or service, only to find that the salesperson misdirected you and you were not satisfied? Perhaps, you did not do your research to prepare yourself to purchase what you were really looking for and you were at the mercy of the salesperson. This is no different in the ski industry. If you do not know how to select the best ski instructor available, you will be handed any coach; some good, some not so good. This book is intended to prepare yourself every step of the way, from how to mentally prepare your child for the first ski lesson, how to dress for the outdoors, preparing for safety, getting the right equipment, what to expect from the first lesson, to how to choose the right coach. No stone will be left unturned; you will be fully prepared for your child's first ski lesson.

CHAPTER 1

Mentally Preparing your Child for Skiing

Not every child is mentally prepared to leave their parents to take their first ski lesson. You may experience separation anxiety. Some will be too young to venture out into the cold to learn how to ski. This chapter will focus on four things:

➢ Determining the proper age to begin this sport.
➢ How to motivate your child to want to learn to ski.
➢ Figuring out what your child wants to learn.
➢ How to assess if your child is mentally, physically, and socially ready to tackle this sport.

Figure 1. *A child that does not want to go skiing, and is pouting because he is not motivated and not mentally prepared to go for a skiing lesson.*

Determining the Proper *Age* to Begin this Sport:

Before we can approach those questions, you need to know about the different developmental stages that a child goes through. We have the Professional Ski Instructors of America (PSIA), who educate, train, and certify instructors in various disciplines, i.e., Alpine skiing, Snowboarding, Cross-country skiing, Free-style Skiing, Adaptive skiing, Telemark skiing, and Children's Specialist skiing. When educating the instructors, they emphasize the importance of using the PSIA **CAP Model**2-[5, 11, 13, 24, 32, 33] when evaluating a student's profile. This model helps the coaches to better understand each child's readiness and to help prepare an appropriate lesson plan, specifically tailor-made to fit your child's profile. It will also help you, as a parent, to better understand the different developmental stages that a child goes through, and what to expect out of a ski lesson. A student-parent coach partnership must develop through constant and proper dialogue for a successful lesson to develop with your child. As a parent, you need to act as your child's consultant and provide sufficient information to the ski instructor so that he/she knows the exact and complete profile of the student. Likewise, the coach needs to provide his/her teaching experiences, his/her goals for your child, and how, where, and when he/she intends to accomplish those objectives. Assessing the student's developmental stages include:

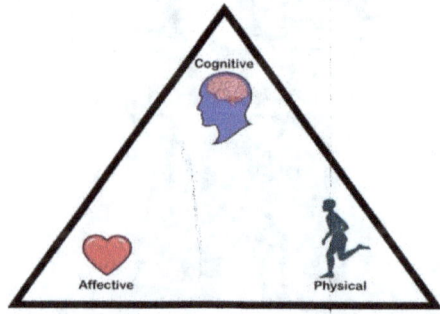

Figure 2. PSIA CAP Model[2-6,13,16,25,30,33]: Cognitive, Affective, and Physical Developments.

Cognitive: How kids think, process the information, follow instructions.

Affective: How kids feel (Humor, how they see themselves, play, follow rules, moral values), how they compete in a sport, how they socialize, and their emotional development.

Physical: How kids move; nerve and skeletal muscle development (Motor control, balance, coordination, large and small muscle movements and coordination).

Cognitive Development:

These stages of *CAP* development will change as your child matures. For example, in the *3- to 6-year-old age group,* they do not understand concrete logic, cannot mentally manipulate information, and are unable to take the point of view of other people. Children become increasingly adept at using symbols, as evidenced by an increase in playing and pretending. For instance, a child is able to use an object to represent something else, such as pretending that a stuffed monkey is a real monkey riding on his/her back. At this age, they often like role-playing like being a policeman, a robber, superman, superwoman, a rabbit hopping around.

Few children show any real understanding of adult conversation prior to the age of five. This age group can only focus on one aspect of a situation at a time. For example, try lining up two rows of pennies in such a way that a row of five pennies is longer than a row of seven pennies. Ask the child to point to the row that has more pennies, and he/she will point to the row of five pennies.

For the 7- *to 10- age group,* the cognitive development is more refined; the brain is more developed. Children demonstrate more independence, self-awareness, and self-confidence. Their vocabulary increases to approximately 2,000 words. They can compose sentences with five or more words. They can count up to 10 objects at one time. They know left from right. They begin to reason and argue and understand concepts like, yesterday, today, and tomorrow. They begin to use words like Why and Because. They can copy complex shapes, such as drawing a diamond, a horse, a bird, a snake. They have more vivid imaginations and can act out the role more realistically. They have a slightly longer attention span and are willing to take on more responsibility. Kids at this age group can tell time, money, days of the week, and read articles of interest.

For the *ages 11- to 18-year-old,* the children begin to verbally, mentally, and physically interact with the world around them. The mental process is more sophisticated and their logic and reasoning are more predominant in the thinking process. With the teens, the information travels faster through the brain and nervous system, resulting in quicker movements and better coordination. By the time they are 16-years old, teens can learn to process more complex problems and more abstract thinking. At this stage, the understanding of their consequences for their deeds or misdeeds is more clearly defined. Advanced mental development may be the result of dramatic brain growth during puberty and then a refining process is seen in the late teen years.

Affective Development:

At this developmental stage, children ***between 3- to 6-years*** begin to understand Right from Wrong. Kids like to acknowledge adults as "All-Knowing" and always doing the right thing. They respect authority as their leaders in their world. Structure in a child's life begins now. Their moral compass begins rapidly. Their emotions are heightened at this stage of growth. That is why we experience Drama Queens with some girls or some boys being exuberant with excitement when given a reward like an ice cream or a birthday gift that they've been wishing for all year long. Children who attended pre-school have an added advantage over those who do not when it comes to communication and socializing with other kids.

The ***7- to 10-year-olds,*** are somewhat innocent and trusting. They believe in Law and Order. They have a perspective that you are still the authority but may have little respect for your intelligence. They may challenge you with some comments that they think that they know more than you. The kids believe in their own cleverness and may disobey adult rules. They are more communicative and more socially inclined to spend more time with other kids. They are willing to share their toys and belongings with others. They are more willing to accept the opinions of others. They have the courage to question your thoughts and commands. They pay more attention to friendships and teamwork. They want to be liked and accepted by their friends. They are better at describing their feelings. They even begin to feel that objects have feelings. Their emotional swings can be greater; tempers can flair, crying can be endless, and joyous experiences can be off the charts. Children in this age group begin to compare himself/herself to other people's expectations. For instance, they love to please their parents and others. They love to mimic others.

The *11- to 18-year- old* children are advancing toward adolescence, and peer friendships start to become a high priority. They tend to cooperate in a group setting and group games and dislike playing alone, especially during the teen years. They spend a lot of time talking with their peers. They develop lasting friendships and begin to handle peer pressures. *As* they mature, they demonstrate growing independence, leading to concern with rules that can lead to bossiness. Teen pressure plays a big role in their behavior. Good and Bad are defined by their social standards. Social acceptance and individual identity are high priorities. They use problem solving, negotiating, and compromising skills with their peers. They start to develop sportsmanship and learn about winning and losing gracefully. They develop a high level of competence in competitive games and in team sports. They become sensitive to what others think of them and seek adult approval. This is the time when clubs and groups become important. They can become critical of their own performances and begin to evaluate themselves. They express subtle emotions and experience moments of anger or frustration. With hormones raging, they can be quite sensitive and overly dramatic; emotions can change quickly. Their self-esteem is extremely critical and be fragile, which may lead to them being shy in public performances. This age group expects others to treat them as if they are fully grown adults. They are very sensitive to criticisms. So, coaches always dwell on the positives and rephrase negative comments to protect their self-esteem.

Physical Development

Children at this *3- to 6-years-old,* start developing from Top to Bottom, and from the core of the body outward to the extremities. The neuromuscular coordination and muscle development are less refined. The large muscles are preferred more than the smaller muscles for movements. Much of the physical movements are governed by the genetic background of the child, by extracurricular experiences, and by preparatory educational background. For instance, if the parents are into sports, their child probably has their athletic genes; if a child has the luxury of attending dance classes, gymnastic classes, or have older brothers or sisters or friends that they play a lot of outdoor games, or have parents that play games with their kids, have better physical development and coordination than those children who do not. The brain is the control center and will fire the impulses down certain neurological pathways for the muscles to respond. The more they use them, the more developed they become. That is why a quarterback has specific drills for the arms and hands, and a running back has specific drills for their leg coordination and movements. In skiing, there are certain neuromuscular pathways that are used more than in other sports. The 3- to 6-yearold children are just beginning to develop some of their neuro-muscular pathways. The right side of the body may not function the same way as the left side. The body matures from top to bottom and from the core outward to the extremities. I do not recommend a child that is less than 2 ½ -years old take lessons. Only under exceptional circumstances, where he/she is extremely athletic, can you consider enrolling him/her into ski school.

The *7- to 10-year-old* students have motor movements that are more refined and their coordination of movements are smoother. They can begin to coordinate one half of the body from the other half with greater ease. Their physical strength and muscle reflexes are advancing. Their range of motion with their extremities shows better coordination with an extended range. Boys and girls develop differently. In general, both genders grow in height and weight at the same slow but steady rate. It is only later (Beyond 10-years old), when the girls start to grow taller and faster, although the boys will catch up and exceed them within a few years.

The 11-*year-old and older age group* have more body strength and hand dexterity. There is improved coordination and faster reaction time. There is an increase in large-muscle coordination, leading to success in organized sports and games. There is also an increase in small-muscle coordination, allowing them to learn complex craft skills; finger control is more refined. There is increased stamina. There is slow and steady muscle growth; the arms are lengthening the hands are growing, legs and feet are getting bigger, stronger, and the different body parts work more smoothly. The nerves are growing with more myelin sheets around the nerves, which speeds up the nerve conduction times for faster muscle reactions. Sometimes the periodic growth spurts can alter their coordination and athleticism, leading to awkwardness. As some parents will say, *"It is unbelievable that it is so common for my son or daughter to stumble over a feather at this stage of development."*

To summarize:

> Does your child have the Cognitive skills to participate in this sport?
> Does he/she have the social skills to be alone with the instructor or participate in a group lesson with other children?
> Do you suspect there will be separation anxiety from you, the parent, and your child when he/she goes out on the snow alone with his ski instructor?
> Does your child have the neuromuscular development to participate in a one-hour or longer ski lesson?
> Children develop at different rates; does your child have the Cognitive, Affective, and Physical developments to ski on a beginner hill?
> Is your child motivated to participate in the skiing learning process?
> Does your child have any developmental disorders that may restrict cognitive, emotional, or bodily functions? Communicate to the coach so he/she is prepared.

Step 2.

Motivating your child:

If you really want your child to ski, you, as a parent, need to take the responsibility to prepare your child for this sport by motivating your child. This can be done by introducing your child to this sport by:

> Reading comic books10,14, 15, 18, 23, 29, 36on skiing adventures to him/her (See photo below). This process will not only entertain your child but will also motivate him/her to want to participate in snow sports.

Photo 1. *After the coloring book session, a coach reads a comic book on skiing to entertain and to motivate the students to want to ski.*

➤ Looking at movies or DVDs on skiing.
➤ Viewing the many Online videos on kids skiing and having a blast on the ski slopes.
➤ Taking him/her to a ski resort to watch an official kids' program *of* that particular age group when it is ongoing at the resort.

With this introduction of information on the different stages of Cognitive Affective and Physical developments, ask yourself the following questions:

➢ Where does your child fit? Be mindful that these are average developmental guidelines. Your child may be above the norm or below the norm. *Genetics,* previous exposure to different athletic programs, and the child's motivations will affect their developmental stages. Obviously, the learning process is generally slower with the younger age groups as compared to the older age groups. Also, try to understand what you can realistically expect[5, 33] for your child to accomplish (See chapter 5). Does your child lean more towards the athletic side, or more to the academic side, or more to the shy and timid side?

➢ Do not hesitate to enroll your 3- or 6-year-old child, even though he/she may be a slower learner or may have a slight disability, as compared to the older kids, i.e., attention-deficit disorder (ADD), attention-deficit-hyperactive disorder (ADHD), or autistic-spectrum disorder (ASD). We have specialized programs for each specific age group and specialized coaches. We even have programs to assist the children with special handicaps (Blind, cognitive impairments, physical impairments); instructors with PSIA certifications for Adaptive Specialist will make it happen. So, do not be hesitant to introduce your child to skiing, it will work; it may just take a little longer to get through the different phases of the learning curve.

Step 3.

Figuring Out What Your Child Wants to Learn:

The parent always knows their child better than anyone else. After going through steps One and Two, does your child want to be a student of the ski school? Or is he/she not quite ready or enthused about this sport? Maybe, he/she have another sport that they're more interested in participating in. Do not force your child into this decision-making process; use a guided discovery method when searching for this answer. What you don't want is a crying child on the slopes because they don't want to be there. You have just wasted time and money without this preparation. Let your child be part of the decision-making process; he/she needs to WANT to be there. Remember, we have many skilled Children's Specialist Coaches that can assist you with this phase of introduction to the sport. A good coach will make every attempt to make your child's first lesson on the snow a fun=filled event and will introduce him/her to an effective skill-learning process (i.e., Edging-, pressure-, rotary-control skills and balance33). You can inform your child of some of the fun activities that he/she will be doing such as making pizzas and French fries, hopping around like crazy jack rabbits, riding scooters, and being a top gun, and superman/superwoman. Many times, I will discover that a two-and-a-half-year-old child is overeager to participate in a skiing lesson, but does not have the cognitive, affective, and physical developments to complete the lesson. I do not generally recommend this age group to take a lesson unless they are exceptionally athletic and super motivated.

Photo 2. *Children are doing foot drills indoors to learn various skiing skills.*

Photo 3. Three-year-old boys are jumping on markers placed on the snow to practice flexing and extending their ankles and knees for pressure control.[33]

13

CHAPTER 2

How to Prepare your Child for the Outdoors

SAFETY15 is always first on the priority list. Teaching a new skill should always be on a proper terrain (i.e., On flat land or less steep of a hill) to promote safety is key to a successful lesson. Doing only drills that will enhance the student's skiing movements in a safe manner to get the skis to respond in a specific way, is also a consideration. After safety, comes *FUN[15]ond LEARNIN&[16]*on the coach's priority list (Observe the snow sports motto).

Also, when communicating with a child, drop to your knees in order to make eye-to-eye contact. This does two things: (1) gets their attention, and (2) they can hear you better because you are closer to their face and you are closer to their ears and they can read your lips. This can be a real safety issue, especially when all the ski guns are making snow and you are wearing an air-borne virus mask. Let me share what I often see; a six-foot instructor standing in front of the child who is three-foot-tall while communicating important instructions. All that the kid sees is two of the coach's kneecaps! How can they hear and bond with the ski instructor?

Photo 4. A coach is on her knees to make eye-to eye contact to
effectively communicate and bond with her students.

Figure 3. *The PSIA has a Snow Sport **Model**:*
Triangle of Safety, Fun, Learning.

Photo 5. You *can generally tell when your student bonded*[16]
with the coach and had a terrific fun lesson by the radiant smile
on the child's face.

Proper Ski Clothing Outfit:

An "ounce of prevention is worth a pound of cure;" do invest in the proper clothing. Dressing with several thin layers is better than one bulky piece of clothing.

Layering properly is noteworthy:

1. *Layer 1* or the *Base Layer*: this is the layer that is next to your skin. It needs to wick the moisture (absorb and move the moisture outward and away from the body), not trap it. Cotton fabric will trap moisture; so, it is not the appropriate fabric to use. Natural fabrics such as wool and silk are the best. Synthetics like polyester blends (i.e., Polypropylene and

16

polyester) are good choices to use. Socks should never be cotton; ski and snowboard socks have special materials that help wick the perspiration from the feet away from the body.

2. *Layer 2* or the Middle Layer: this mid-layer is the workhorse. Traditionally this layer is bulky because it has the job of holding warm air, which is the best insulator and moving the wicked moisture from the first layer. Technology has advanced so much that many of today's fabrics are now thinner. Non-pulling fleece or wool Sweaters or turtlenecks are great options.

3. *Layer 3* or the Outer Layer: this layer is the shell (Jacket or trousers) that should keep out the rain, wind, and snow. Many manufacturers print the IP rating on the marketing tags, i.e., 5,000 mm to 20,000 mm. Higher the rating, the higher the waterproofing and breathability of the garment. There are special tricks when buying pants; there are some brands that have adjustable hems that can be adjusted to the proper length as their kids grow.

➤ Don't forget the face mask and/or Balaklava to protect the face from the cold and COVID-19 virus. Today, the manufacturers have been more creative to make translucent face masks to allow you to see one's facial expression.

➤ No matter how warm the temperature will be, be sure that the gloves will be warm enough and that it is water-proof.

➤ When preparing your child for their first ski lesson, you need to check the oncoming weather forecast. What is the forecast for the amount of snow that was dumped on the ground and how much more do you expect? What is the temperature going to be when your child has the advanced-booked lesson? What will the wind-chill factor be? Will it be blizzard-like conditions? How much wind will there be? Will it be raining? Will there be any sunshine?

Photo 6. *Three children are prepared for the cold weather because they are properly dressed. They are also having fun because they are making snowballs.*

Photo 7. Do not underestimate the temperature, especially the low wind-chill factor; these kids are properly dressed. They and their coaches are sitting on the snow doing foot drills (Making pizzas and French fries) for rotary-control skills.

CHAPTER 3

Getting the Proper Equipment

Gathering your child's ski equipment can always be a daunting task. Where do you go? What do you get? What specifications do I need to know? Don't fret, I am going to recommend the essentials and what to look for so that you're better prepared.

Proper Skis:

➤ Most of today's skis at the rental shops are shaped for easier turning. You can use the older straight-shaped skis, but I do not recommend it; the teaching is slightly different from shaped skis and it is harder to maneuver and turn.

➤ Ski length is paramount for the beginner skier. Most of the rental shops will provide skis that have a length from the ground up to the tip of the skis that *reaches* somewhere between the chin and nose. That's basically the standard length. I recommend shorter lengths for easier maneuverability; somewhere between the lower sternum to the chin. Be sure to tell the rental shop employee that he/she is a beginner skier; you definitely want shorter skis per the coach's recommendation.

Proper Helmet:

A common cause of injury in the Snow Sports industry is falling down and/or being hit by someone else, or even your child hitting an object or someone. Helmets have been documented to reduce the incidence of any head injury by 30-50 percent, but the *decrease* in head injuries is generally limited to less serious injuries, such as scalp lacerations, and mild concussions (Grade I), and contusions. Helmets are presently not designed for more serious injuries like a concussion greater than Grade II, skull fractures, open head injuries, and the like. Be aware that once your child gets a concussion, he/she is five times more likely to get another. Unfortunately, a person colliding with your child is about 6.4% of the reported accidents to the Ski Patrol. Who knows the number of unreported cases? According to the 2009-2020 National Ski Areas Association, 57% of Snow Sports enthusiasts use helmets. The data also show that 97% of children 9-years or younger are wearing helmets; 75 percent of children between 10-14 years wear helmets. So, someday the ski resorts will make it mandatory to wear helmets, especially when going into the Terrain Parks.

> ➢ Helmets can help protect your child's brain. They cost somewhere between $50-350. The more expensive helmets generally have added features, such as better insulation, better ear covering that allow sound to access the ear, adjustable air vents, and others. How much should you spend? Well, it all depends on how much you value your child's brain.

> ➢ Make sure that the helmet is approved by CEN 1077, SSTM, or Snell organizations to ensure performance standards and impact specifications. Snell has the highest standards, while CEN has the lowest approved standards.

> Research and development are continuously discovering new materials that can better absorb impacts and new designs that can be more protective. For instance, some manufactures use Back Protectors or Bumper that are molded to the body of the helmet and also provide more comfort. Other manufacturers design helmets with MIPS©, which stands for Multidirectional Impact Protection System. It is designed to redirect and reduce the impact, even from an indirect hit. The MIPS© involves a low-friction layer inside the helmet over which the outer helmet moves after the impact. As helmets evolve, the manufacturers will offer helmets that can reduce concussions.

> Helmets have a limited life span. According to research data, after several collisions, it may be deemed less effective.

> Do not use hand-me-down helmets from older children or receive an old helmet from another family.

> Helmets come in various styles and shapes. Among these are the full shell, ¾shell, and full-faced models.

> Full shell models provide more coverage (Including the ears) and protection, but they can get hot on warmer days. Remember that a child will lose 60% of their body heat from their head. Thus, you would be wise to purchase a helmet with adjustable air vents.

> Comfort and fit are both important when selecting a helmet. The fit should be snug, but not tight. I see too often, a child with an inappropriate fitted helmet that sits above the front hairline; a properly fitted helmet should cover the frontal lobe (Halfway down the forehead). That child with the helmet resting just above the front hairline has probably outgrown the helmet.

> Color may be important to your child to match the ski outfit that you purchased; but, a more important consideration should be

visible to others on the slope. You may want to select a color that is unique and bright; i.e., Orange or Lime Green, instead of the standard Black, Grey, or White.

Proper Ski Goggles:

➢ Not all ski goggles have the same contour to match the contour of your child's face and the contour of the helmet you selected. While you're in the ski shop purchasing a helmet, you may want to consider buying a ski goggle that matches the front contour of your helmet. There should be no gaps between the top of the goggle and the helmet. The strap of the goggle must be able to go outside the helmet, where it can be attached to a devicc at the back of the helmet (To prevent run-away gear).

➢ The goggles will not only help protect the eyes from the cold, wind, sun, and snow but give added protection from injury from the sun. Lens choices are many. VTL or the amount of light that passes through the lenses and *reaches* your eyes. The color of your lens can affect the percentage of VTL reaching your eyes. They are usually clear or a very light tinted grey that can be used with highly overcast skies or at night. There are also VTL lenses that are 25% or less, which can be used for slightly overcast or cloudy skies. They have VTL lenses that are 50% or greater; they come in yellow, gold/copper, amber, or rose-colored. Then, there are specialized lenses with enhancing lens technology to help you to see details on the snow to respond quicker to the terrain conditions.

➢ There are specific dyes used in the lenses, which manipulate the light spectrum to filter out "noisy colors", while simultaneously enhancing the color that your eyes are responsive to. Some of the high-end lenses used in the industry are truly remarkable. The lens technology has advanced to the point that some high-tech lenses will automatically change from low VTL or high VTL.

> Goggle safety also includes the effectiveness of fog removal; this is accomplished by a well-designed goggle that has enough vents to remove the fog from the inside of the *goggle* when your head

> heats up and produces the fog in the cold weather. Some goggles do a better job as compared to other less expensive ones.

> Most goggles have a thin anti-fog coating on the inside of the lens. Do not rub the inside of the lens when it gets wet, with an abrasive towel. This will not only scratch the lens but also remove the thin anti-fog coating. Just let the goggles air dry or use the lens cloth that the manufacturer provided.

Proper Ski Boots:

Ski Boots are the most important ski gear. Safety can be an issue if they are improperly fitted. All too often, a parent will get hand-me-downs, or purchase one at a swap meet, or obtain one at a second-hand store. Most of the time they are too big! In an oversized boot, the kid can be swimming in those monstrous clunkers, thus, resulting in their foot to "swim" all over the place, which causes imbalance during their movements to turn the skis. This leads to ineffective skiing and is a safety risk for falling. In addition, a loosely fitted boot will *decrease* the response time for edge-to-edge maneuvers because of the delay of movements in the boots.

> The boots should fit snuggly, but not tightly, creating no pain. Educate your child what snug fit means; do a handshake and grip his/her hand firmly, short of pain. That's what his/her foot should feel like when you buckle down.

> If you're purchasing a boot, get them from a skilled boot fitter. It certainly is an art and a science. The shell comes in full sizes and

the liner in half sizes. The foot is measured with a special tool and is usually marked in Mondo sizes:

USA Kids Sizes	Mondo Sizes
7	13.5
8	14.5
9	15.5
10	16.5
11	17.5
12	18.5
13	19.5
1	20.5
2	21.5
3	22.0
4.5	22.5
5	23.0
5.5	23.5
6.0	24.0
7.0	24.5
8.0	25.5
9.0	26.5

Table 1. Boot Sizes

A skilled boot fitter will always first do a shell fit by removing the boot liner and having the child place his/her foot into the boot while standing up. The toes should just touch the front toe of the boot. The boot fitter will check if there is one-finger width on either side of the foot and a two-finger width behind the heel, which leaves room for the growing child. The boot liner will take up one-finger width when placed back into the boot shell. To get the heel to slide back into the heel pocket, the child, while sitting down, should firmly tap the heel onto the floor at an angle. Then clamp down on the buckle closest to the ankles; then, do the rest of the buckles and the power strap (If there is one).

Have the person stand and flex the boot like they are in an athletic stance.[33] If the toes pull back from the front of the boot, it is a properly fitted boot.

Photo 8. *A* three-year-old girl in ski boots that are slightly too large. You think!

Proper Ski Poles:

For a beginner, the poles are *not* recommended because of the possible distraction of the tiny tikes during skiing and also poses difficulty when getting on to the chairlift. It is only when they reach towards the end of the intermediate zone, that the coach will ask you to get ski poles.

The proper size of the ski poles should be determined by holding the ski poles upside down; then gripping just under the ski basket. It is a proper fit if the forearm is parallel to the ground.

> While slightly more expensive, you might want to consider adjustable ski poles. In the long run, you will save money, instead of purchasing new poles at each stage of his/her growth.
> Place an address label (With a telephone number) somewhere on the poles in case they are forgotten at the ski school.
> Poles can be dangerous; teach your child to never point the basket end towards anyone in front of them. It can become a weapon!

Photo 9. *This ten-year-old boy is not ready for ski poles because he is distracted, and drops his arms, hands, and poles. This causes him to be out of balance because his COM is behind his BOS.*

CHAPTER 4

Preparing for Safety

Safety is the highest priority in every ski instructor's mind. There are many safety rules on the hill that the coach will focus on when providing his/her first lesson and will continue to do so throughout their lessons. There are over 300 million Snow Sports enthusiasts throughout the world and accidents do happen. It is estimated that over 600,000 injuries are reported each year nationally, as a result of skiing and snowboarding. For this chapter, I will focus on what you can do to prepare your child for their first lesson. I mentioned in chapter 2 how to dress your child appropriately for the cold weather. The major safety *concerns* for your child are the safety policies that keep changing at each ski resort for COVID-19. With the viral air-born pandemic, the ski industry is going through a major revolution for safety.[19]

In conjunction with the National Ski Areas Association (NSSA) and PSIA/AASI encourages everyone to follow the national guidelines, "Ski Well, Be Well" (nsaa.org@skiwellbewell[20]). See photo 53. Review the periodic Guidelines for Safety updates that are aligned with the Centers For Disease Control and Prevention (tiny.cc@covid-19cdcquidelines[20]). This is your responsibility too! A there are other issues that you need to consider as a responsible parent before you send your child out for the first lesson:

- ➢ Is your child properly fed[24,37,] and hydrated.[24,37]
- ➢ Did your child receive his/her medications[24,37]?
- ➢ Is your child properly dressed for the on-coming weather?
- ➢ Did your child go to the bathroom just before the ski lesson?
- ➢ Did you avoid booking your toddler's ski lesson during his/her typical nap time?
- ➢ Do you have any safety or medical concerns that the coach needs to know?

The weather is not predictable in many parts of the country; it can change in a heartbeat and turn nasty. Because of this phenomenon, I have experienced many unforgiving weather conditions. I would like to spend some time in this chapter to discuss *frostbite.* This is a common and serious problem. Children are particularly susceptible because of several reasons:

- ➢ Children lose heat from their skin (Particularly from their heads) much faster than adults.
- ➢ Kids can get so excited and engrossed in playing in the snow that they lose track of what is happening to their bodies or simply ignore how cold or uncomfortable they are and continue having uninterrupted fun with their friends.
- ➢ A three- or four- or even five-year-old child may not have the skills to alert them to the symptoms of frostbite or when to take a break and seek warm shelter. A ski instructor will, but you should educate your child to recognize the symptoms.

Frostbite refers to the freezing of the body's skin and underlying tissues that is caused by extreme cold. There are three degrees of frostbite:

> *Frostnip.* white patches of skin that are numb.

> *Superficial frostbite*: skin that is white and hard; deep skin, blood vessels, and nerve injury with a burning and stinging sensation; clear water-filled blisters that may develop when the skin is re-warmed.

> *beep frostbite*: Grayish-yellow or blue skin and feels hard or waxy; larger blood vessels and nerves, muscles, tendons, and bone injury occur with the loss of sensation; gangrene and infections may develop.

So, what should you do? As a parent, *prevention* is key. Recognize the symptoms and take action quickly. Educate your child on what to feel and look for when it is bitter cold. Check the exposed areas of the skin; is there redness, or any other color change, or lack of color? A frostnip skin starts out being red and later turns pale, cold, and hard with no feelings. Does he/she feel "pins and needles"? This sensation is followed by numbness and this may lead to an early throbbing or aching feeling; but, later on, the affected part feels like a "block of wood." Alarm signals are:

> *Are* they feeling cold? *Are* they beginning to shiver? How do their finger and toes feel? They need to come in immediately. The most common areas of the body that are affected are the finger and toes (Which account for 90 percent of the cases), nose, lips, cheeks, and ears.

> Some medical conditions such as peripheral vascular disease, Renaud's Syndrome, hypothyroidism (Low thyroid function), heart problems can result in increased susceptibility to frostbites.

> Once you get frostbitten, you are 5 times more like to get another one. So, be on the lookout if you had one.

Here is a summary of *frostbite symptoms*:

➤ Redness of the skin
➤ Loss of skin color
➤ Blue skin color
➤ Shivering
➤ Slurred speech
➤ Graying of the skin
➤ Feeling Pins and Needles
➤ Local numbness
➤ Local blisters
➤ Local swelling
➤ Memory loss

I should mention that a child with frostbite on the extremities may also be subjected to hypothermia (Lowered body core temperature). Check for hypothermia and treat these symptoms first. Remove all wet clothing and provide warmth. How do you proceed with the **treatment** of frostbite? Work quickly:

➤ Get your child out of the wind and cold immediately
➤ Move to a warm shelter
➤ Remove any wet or damp clothing, mittens, and socks
➤ Remove any constricting jewelry
➤ Remove any tight clothing or clothing that may restrict blood flow (i.e., Belt, jackets with elastic wrist band)
➤ Apply slow warming with blankets and warm clothing
➤ Do *NOT* rub or massage the frostbitten areas
➤ bo *NOT* let the child walk on the frostbitten feet
➤ bo *NOT* apply any direct heat to the area

- ➤ bo *NOT* sit by the fireplace to warm up
- ➤ bo *NOT warm* the child with an electric blanket
- ➤ bo *NOT* break the blisters
- ➤ bo provide ample warm fluids
- ➤ Preventive antibiotic medications may be necessary per the advice of the doctor
- ➤ Pain medications may be necessary if recommended by the do
- ➤ Treatment for general hypothermia may be necessary

So, common sense should dictate when your child should come into a warmer environment. Proper behavioral changes are imperative through proper education.

Allergies:

I bring this topic up because many of the food consumed at the food court at the resort are catered or homemade and one cannot read the labels. Allergies are a growing problem and concern. This is a condition in which a person's immune system overreacts to substances known as *allergens* and releases a chemical called histamines, which causes the symptom. A common source of allergens is:

- ➤ *Foods*: nuts (Peanuts, cashews, walnuts), shellfish (Shrimp, lobster, crab), fish, sesame seeds (Commonly found in bagels and Asian foods), certain legumes (Lentils, peas, soybeans), dairy (Milk, eggs) are very common.
- ➤ *Insects*: many flying insects (Stings from honeybees, yellow jackets, wasps, hornets) ants, ticks can cause severe allergies.
- ➤ *Medications*: penicillin and many antibiotics, chemotherapy, muscle relaxants, pain relievers (Aspirin, ibuprofen, non-steroidal

32

and anti-inflammatory drugs, latex-related products (Balloons, gloves) are common allergens.

- *Contact dermatitis*: clothing (Certain natural fabrics and dyes) is common.
- *Pollens*: many trees, weeds, plants, and grasses release pollens that will cause hay fever.
- *Mold and dust mites*: *are* the biggest allergy triggers in the Fall.
- *Animals:* the fur or hairs, saliva, urine, and dander (Dried flakes or skin) are common culprits.

Many of the allergies can be benign, and others can be life-threatening. Let's look at the *symptoms* presented by these two categories:

A. **Benign symptoms:**
- Nasal congestion
- Itchy and watery eyes
- Sneezing
- Stuffy or runny nose
- Scratchy or sore throat
- Cough from post-nasal drip
- Flam
- Drowsiness

B. **Life-threatening allergies—Anaphylaxis warning signs:**
- Breathing difficulties
- Low blood pressure
- Change in consciousness
- Chest pain or tightness of chest and trouble swallowing

- Hives, swelling of the lips and other areas of the body, a tingling feeling, itchiness, or skin rash
- Nausea, vomiting, dizziness, diarrhea, and stomach cramps

One needs to respond swiftly if you recognize some of these *life-threatening symptoms:*

- Do you carry an epinephrin pen? Do you know how to use it?
- *Go* to the Ski Patrol desk or to the hospital or clinic's emergency room.
- Have your child carry an epinephrin pen and inform his/her coach where it is located.

"Ski Resorts Adjust, Hope Season Gets a Longer Run," in USA Today, November 19, 2020, page 4D.

CHAPTER 5

What to Expect from Your Child's First Ski Lesson?

Parents should always have goals for their children when they *go for* the child's first ski lesson. Parents always tend to expect the most out of a lesson. But is it realistic? Is it beyond your child's capabilities? *A better way you should view this:*

> ➢ *Are my* expectations realistic?
> ➢ Can my child achieve those goals?
> ➢ The coach will be able to separate ***Ideal***[4, 16] goals from ***Realistic*** [4, 16] goals.

The last thing that you want to do is to set up ideal goals that are not achievable. You will be disappointed at the outcome of the child's first lesson, and your child will be unhappy because he/she was not able to please you with 100 percent customer satisfaction[22] Worse yet, his/her self-esteem and self-confidence may be compromised. The coach's goal is to always preserve the child's confidence and self-esteem at all cost. Always remember, children always seek parents' approval and performance satisfaction as a reward for their efforts and build confidence and self-esteem. With this negative scenario, it will be difficult to motivate a student to continue with this sport with enthusiasm.

So, what is a realistic[4,16] goal for the first lesson? Always be aware that the parents and sometimes the child has unrealistic goals. It is the coach's job to realign the expectations and keep the goals realistic. The following is an example:

What to Expect for a Three- to six-Year-Old Student

Before the ski lesson:

- An introduction by your child's coach—his background, his experiences as an instructor, and the objectives for the day.
- Your instructor might check if your child is properly dressed, check if his/her boots are put on correctly, and whether or not he/she has the proper ski equipment.
- This might include explaining the parts of the ski and what their functions are. We will start the teaching process in a wedge platform because it is more stable than a parallel platform and the child will go slower, which is safer than the faster parallel platform.
- This might include where they'll be skiing. The coach should selecta slower grade hill for safety reasons.

Figure 4. *a wedge (Pizza) and another skier is in a parallel (French fries) platform.*

➢ The coach might have a safety[16]checklist that he/she might want to go through the ABCs of safety.

1. *A* = Above: Always be visible to skiers above you.

2. *B* = *Breaks:* Be sure to have *ski brakes* working and retention strap on your skis poles to prevent runaway equipment.

3. *C* = *Control:* Be sure you ski in *control* at all times.

4. **D**= Downhill: The *downhill* skier has the right-of-way; do not collide into them, if you are going to overtake them, say out loud, *"Skier on your left or right."*

5. **E**= Enter: *Enter* trails safely—whenever starting downhill or merging on a new trail, always *look uphill* and yield.

6. **F**= Follow: *Follow* all *posted signs, stay* off of *closed trails.*

7. *G*= *Get: Get on and* off the chairlifts safely. Know how to load, ride and unload the *chair and conveyer belt* properly and safely.

> ➤ This might also include what he/she hope to accomplish during their lesson period. *A* major goal is should be on achieving *balance*[33] on the skis during movements. The ski runs should be gentle and short to maximize safety for the child. Homework should be focused on learning the three skills and balance. *A* great fun exercise for balance is the flamingo exercise.

Figure 5. *The flamingo drill: lifting a leg and seeing how long the child can be balanced on the other leg.*

38

Photo 10. This is a fun game to do because the children and coaches are lifting one leg and seeing how long they can maintain balance on the other leg. (Was photo 28)

Photo 11. Children and coaches are lifting one ski off the snow and balancing[4, 33] on the other ski.

➢ Has the child eaten,[24, 37] is hydrated[24, 37], taken his/her medication[24, 37] went to the bathroom before the lesson,[24, 37] and feel protected and *safe[24, 37]* Physilogical needs must always be met while skiing.

➢ The coach may explain where you'll be training and where you'll be delivered to your parents.

➢ The emphases of the lesson will be having fun and building *trust* and *bonding.15* This is paramount to good coaching. Without these two key ingredients, your child may not enjoy taking lessons and may not be on the fast track to learning the fundamentals of skiing. So, how can the ski instructor develop bonding and trust? What are some of the clues that you can look for examining the coach's creativity and ingenuity when establishing that connection? Examine your own experiences when you got your first pet? Your first clue to the importance of developing bonding and trust is to observe if you can get the animal to respond to your command. Or a newborn child will not immediately gravitate to you unless you tempt the child with food or something rewarding.

Photo 12. *An extremely happy thirteen-year-old girl because she bonded with her coach and had a ton of fun on and off the slopes.*

➤ Over the years, I met four equine students who wanted to learn skiing. I curiously communicated with them and did a lot of *research on* horse-riding training.[26,32, 38]You know, "There are a lot of similarities when teaching a child to ski with training people to ride a horse:

- You cannot ride a horse before developing a relationship with the horse; one must develop bonding and trust with the horse before riding it is crucial. Same with kids, the coach needs to have a good relationship with the child through bonding and trust.

- The bonding needs to be reinforced frequently by gentle verbal communications, with warm body gestures (Rubbing the nose, forehead, neck area, called "Horse handshake") and giving rewards (i.e., Carrots, apples, and other treats). If a coach wants to maintain that bond, he/she needs to reinforce it with gentle, positive words and give ample high-fives, hugs, and verbal praises.

- Safety is a high priority; the horse wants to always be in a safe environment. The rider will wear a helmet and riding boots. Children will wear the proper ski boots, helmets, and clothing.

- Going slow before you ride faster (Walk, trot, canter, gallop) is always suggested; likewise, skiing on safe and gentle terrain slowly is recommended before skiing on steep and fast terrain.

- Learning to ride in a balanced position in the saddle is required before learning other fundamental movements; likewise, in skiing we want the student to master balance throughout the turns on the hills of different steepness.

- The rider is required to be in synchronization and alignment with the galloping horse's rhythm; just as a skier's core (Center of Mass) needs to be in alignment with his/her feet (Base of Support).

- *A* horse does not want to be treated roughly, or yelled at, or too tightly controlled; neither does a student.

I relish the moments when I have students that have horse-riding skills as a hobby. I go into horse-training mode. The learning curve is much faster because the students understand the fundamentals of riding the horse, which is similar to the fundamentals of skiing.

I share with you this information because it can help you find a better ski coach. How?

By looking for the creativity and ingenuity in a coach. The coach's job is to develop a lesson plan that will unlock your student's interest, motivation, and excitement about wanting to learn everything about skiing. To find the key to the lock, you need to discover where the key is located by asking a lot of creative questions, like what kind of sports, movies, or hobbies that they like to participate in? If I find a student that is familiar with horse riding, I certainly use the horse-riding technique and approach to teach skiing. The learning curve is much quicker with students with equine knowledge. If your student does not have an interest in horse-riding, I hope that his/her coach finds a sport or hobby that he/she can find ways to build a solid skiing platform by integrating the Five Fundamentals of Skiing Model.[33]

As a member of the *Educational Staff* at our three resorts in Ohio, I always marvel at the ski instructors who decided to take to heart what they learned in the many workshops and clinics; and implemented the skills, fundamentals, and tips into their lesson plans with more parental, customer, other coach's praises and rewards. The outcome of this effort is:

(1) They have many private requests,

(2)   They get more monetary rewards,

(3) They get more requests from the new-heir coaches to shadow them.

There is a lot of time and effort that a coach must invest when establishing a connection with a child. Without *bonding* and *trust,* the process of learning becomes an uphill battle. Bonding and trust should start with the children's parents, quickly followed by the child. The parent is the Customer (The decision-maker and the payee) and the child is the Consumer (Will consume what the coach hands to him/her).

1. Good connection starts with communicating with your eyes; observe if the ski instructor drops to his/her knees to make eye contact with your child's eyes. (See photo 4).

During the Ski Lesson (one hour):

➢ For a one-hour lesson, you should expect your 3- *to 6-year-old* child should to be on flat land, scooting around on one ski making figure 8s and circles in both directions (See photo 13). They should be able to make a pizza (Wedge) and French fries (Parallel) with their boots and then with their skis. They should be able to make J- and C-Turns off a 3- or 4-foot runoff hill. Depending on their age, athleticism, and other factors, he/she may be able to do linked wedge turns (See photo 36). On their first lesson, they should immediately be taught how to carry their own skis (See photo 13), unless you wish to carry your child's skis! I tell the kids, "To stretch your arms out and carry the skis like carrying a baby."

Photo 13. *A three-year-old munchkin is carrying her own skis properly and safely.*

➢ Not every day is a perfect learning day; your child may not be on her best performance for whatever reason. The student may not care for the coach; they didn't connect. The snow conditions or snow texture may not be the best that day.

Photo 14. *Not every day is a beautiful walk in the park; this three-year-old girl, an excellent skier, may be having a bad-hair day with her new coach. Every ski instructor should expect the unexpected; always be prepared to address the issues and bring on happy faces.*

➤ A great coach is an entertainer who *creates fun* times on the hill and off the hill. Has the ski instructor spent the time to be a magician,[21,28]a ventriloquist,[32]or gifted enough to be a singer?

Photo 15. *A coach (ventriloquist) is entertaining a three-year-old boy with a hand puppet for entertainment and to build bonding and trust.*

Photo 16. *A ski instructor is trying to establish a bond and trust with a young girl by entertaining her with a magic trick.*

➢ Allow me to give an example of how magical tricks assisted me with a kid who didn't appear to care to take a skiing lesson. To illustrate how powerful this can be, I will share with you a story about a four-year girl, Abigayle, who came to the ski resort for her first ski lesson. She and her dad were at the ski-school registration desk to book a lesson with me. I realized she was stuttering whenever she tried to talk. I also realized that I need to calm her anxiety so she wouldn't be embarrassed during her lesson and by people around her. While on both knees, I told Abigayle that, "I

48

had magical powers to always keep her safe and promised her that we were going to have tons of fun on the snow. I showed her my powers by demonstrating two different magical tricks (One: two red-color balls, one in each of my hands disappeared before her vary eyes; two: a disappearing in a small bag when I said, "abracadabra, disappear!" She was in awe, only to find the blue ball in her ski jacket pocket! She took my hand and we walked out to the snow while I carried her skis. We hopped on one leg on flat land, pretending that we both had a broken left ankle from a bicycle accident the previous week. The purpose was for weight transfer to the right foot and to see how long we can be balanced on one foot. Then we switched to the other leg and also timed our balance on each flamingo stance. The right leg was stronger and more coordinated. I asked her, "Are you right-handed or left-handed?"

"What do you think?"

Then, we started with a static drill by making smiley faces in the snow with her right foot and then with her left boot to familiarize her with edge control.*33*I demonstrated the perfect size pizza (Being hip width) and then I demonstrated a perfect size French fries (Being hip width).

We went to a five-foot runoff and glided down in a wedge platform. During this time, I was able to assess her PSIA *CAP* developments; 0 to 10 (10 Being the best). Her Cognitive development was a 10, her Affective development was an 8, and her Physical development was a 9. Based on those numbers, I developed a lesson plan tailored to her needs.

Towards the end of the one-hour lesson, we moved higher on the slope, six-foot, seven-foot, and ten-foot runoffs—all the while assessing her movement skills, and how they affected the skis. Whenever I saw a technical error, I informed Abigayle how we could do it better without being negative. I sprinkled a little humor periodically by making kids' jokes to get her to relax and have fun during the lesson. She did gliding-wedge runs with slightly larger pizzas (Wedge-changeups) at the bottom to get her to stop. I get a little concerned with this method of stopping because too large of a wedge was causing her *COM* to be slightly behind the BOS, which resulted in her being slightly out of balance,[33]thus causing imbalance. I prefer J-turns to make stops. Abigayle couldn't do Jturns, so we stuck with a slightly larger wedge to come to a complete stop on a slightly steep hill. This technique later proved to be useful for emergency stops. She was tickled pink and we went to the ski lodge and commented to her dad What, Where, How, and Why we did those drills. I asked Abigayle, "What she thought of her first ski lesson?"

She said, "I loved it; it was better than riding my bicycle!"

I gave the smiling Abigayle homework on rotary control[33]by doing pizza and French fries on paper plate under each barefoot on the carpet to maximize the ease of turning the plates. If a marble, wooden, or linoleum floor is used, sprinkle a little baby powder under the paper plate to make the rotational turns easier.

I gave Abigayle a second homework because she had difficulty making J-turns come to a stop. With the consent of the parents, I told them that this exercise is a little messy. Place a large marshmallow under her arch and toes, and have her squash them until they are flat for edging- and pressure-control.

At the end of the lesson, I rewarded Abigayle with a candy Kiss (With the approval of her dad). I then did a magic trick of the disappearing nickel in the box and found the lost nickel in her ski jacket pocket. I was booked every weekend with Abigayle for the rest of the ski season.

Photo 17. *A three-year-old girl showing excitement and joy after completing her first-ski lesson. This positive outcome of overwhelming happiness is the result of good coaching.*

➤ *A* creative coach uses a lot of ski tools and games to make the lessons easier and more fun. Observe which ski instructors are creative.

Photo 18. *A three-year-old girl is using a ski-tip connector to help her make and maintain a wedge platform*

Photo 19. *A three-year-old girl with her hands on each knee to her to turn by pushing both knees in the direction of the turn.*

Photo 20. *A four-year-old girl is scooting around on her "Scooter" (Ski) to practice weight transfer and pressure control on the one scooter while maintaining balance.*[4, 33]

➤ Depending on their age, some children may be able to do some directional change in a pizza, going down the three- to four-foot runoff (A small and short hill). One of the primary goals of an instructor is having his students make perfect wedge turns. But the ski instructor must focus on first attaining a perfect athletic stance to be in perfect balance. This is achieved by the child's *COM* (Hip and upper body) is over the BOS (Arches of the feet). A good thing to remember is "to have his knees ahead of the child's toes, and the child's knees ahead of the child's toes, and having the nose ahead of the child's knees by bending at the hip. Without being in a balanced position on those skis, the other skills (Edging-, pressure-, and rotary control cannot be achieved. There will be days when nothing seems to be working. A seasoned coach will have the experience and training to visually spot cues when the child's alignment is not correct. Take for instance in Photo 23 where this boy's lateral alignment is not balanced on the skis. The solution to this challenge is to keep working on the fundamentals of balancing and to have patience—lots of patience. Having a trained eye for spotting cues that indicate improper movements is important and critical. Like in medicine, without the proper diagnosis, one cannot correct the problem.

Photo 21. A *three-year-old girl with an excellent balance through good athletic stance.*[6, 33]

Photo 22. *An eleven-year-old girl with excellent balance because of her excellent athletic stance*[6, 33]*while skiing.*

Photo 23. This young lad is out of balance because there is unequal weight distribution over both skis. Without the proper athletic stance, the young boy will have difficulties implementing the other skiing skills.6, 33

➢ Many 3- to 6-year-old children cannot climb the hill by themselves. They need to learn doing side-steps, or the herringbone walk or have the assistance of ski tools like the plastic hoop.

Photo 24. *A three-year-old boy is being assisted by his coach as he learns the side-step movement up the homemade ramp with a carpet indoors for an easier climb up the ramp.*

Photo 25. *A shy four-year-old girl practicing her herringbone walk on flat land before attempting to climb the hill. To climb the hill, she will be encouraged to make bigger ice-cream cones to create more edge angles for better traction.*

Photo 26. *A four-year-old boy is being pulled up the hill by his coach with a plastic hoop.*

.

➤ The major focus of every lesson should be on getting your child into an athletic *stance5, 33*for better balance (See photos 8, 10, 21, 22, 42, 43, 52).

➤ Your child will fall at least once during his/her lifetime while on the snow. The instructor will show your child to get up off the snow by themselves. It may take a few times to fully understand the steps needed to accomplish this. Falling is usually the result of being out of balance (See photos 9, 23, 34).

Photo 27. *A young girl is getting up after a fall, by rolling over onto a prone position and pushing herself backward until she is upright.*

➤ Learning how to fit his/her boots into the ski bindings and how to get out of the ski bindings will be taught.

60

➢ A major objective is to provide fun activities for your child, while still learning proper body movements for skiing.

Photo 28. *A three-year-old girl is flexing her ankles and knees and bending from her hip to get shorter as she goes under the bridge.*

After the Ski Lesson

➢ At the end of the lesson, the coach will provide a summary of *what* your child was taught, *why* he/she did those drills, and *how* and *where* he/she did those drills. An overall critique of your child's performance will be given. For the next lesson, the coach will expound on what he/she will be working on to improve the body movements to get the skis to respond in a more appropriate manner.

➢ The child may receive a reward such as a sticker to be placed on his/her helmet or skis. That will be his/her badge of honor for doing good work on the slopes.

➢ Your child may receive homework to better for the next lesson. For instance, doing the flamingo drill by balancing on one leg while lifting the other. This balancing exercise can be enhanced by making it more fun by timing how long each leg can be raised. One leg is usually stronger and more coordinated than the other. The child's parents can inform you of the results of the homework.

Another homework that works is making pizzas and French fries while his/her barefoot are on paper plates that are placed on a carpet for easier rotational movements. If you are ambitious, you may want to construct a balance beam by purchasing a 4" x 4" x 8' lumber, and attaching a 4" x 4" x 4' piece on either end of the beam for stability. It has been my experience as a coach that if a student is taking a gymnastic class, they always have better balance skills for skiing.

➢ The coach should be able to inform you what you and your child can expect for the next lesson, (i.e., Learning how to do the different kinds of turn shapes to control the speed down the hill). They will also be told how wedges allow the skier to go at a slower speed as compared to a parallel platform-larger the wedge the slower your child will go. In addition, different turn shapes will also affect speed. An S-turn will make a skier go faster as compared to a C-turn or a J-turn.

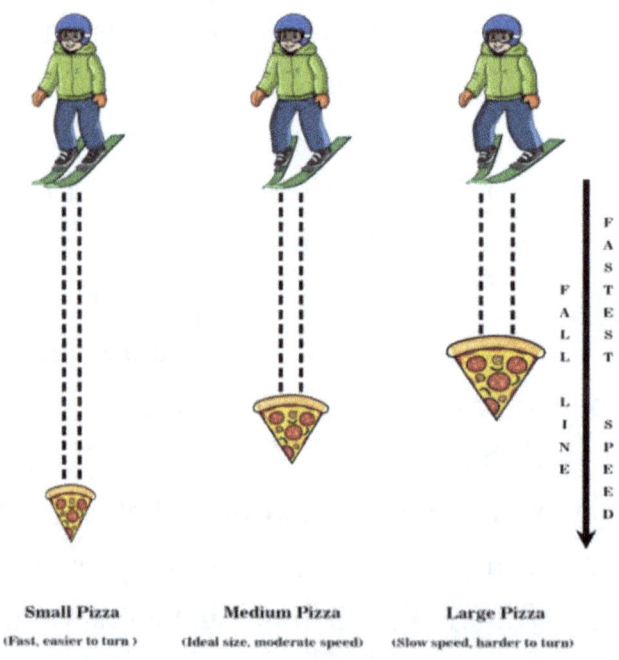

Small Pizza
(Fast, easier to turn)

Medium Pizza
(Ideal size, moderate speed)

Large Pizza
(Slow speed, harder to turn)

Figure 6. *Different size pizzas will influence speed.*[3, 12, 25]

Figure 7. *Three different turn shapes that affect speed.3, 12, 25*

Figure 8. *Different size wedges and parallel platforms will affect speed.* [3, 12, 25]

➢ One of the things that I tell my students is, *"Speed causes injuries. That is why they have safe speed limits in the city and on the highways. When your parents exceed the speed limits, they can get a speeding ticket and you can get one too from the snow patrol. So, always ski safely by going slow."* So, how do you do *Speed Control?*

• Wedges go slower than parallel skiing.

• The larger the wedge the slower you go.

• Finish your turns.

• Select the proper terrain. Do not select a terrain that is beyond the child's capabilities.

- The shape of the turns matters:

  1. J-turns is the slowest because the upward turn of the last part of the "J" goes against gravity, which actually makes you stop.
  2. C-turns allow you to link the turns and go down the hill in a slow speed.
  3. The S-turn is a faster way to go down the slope.

- ➤ A parallel platform is the fastest way to go down the hill..
- ➤ *A* coach with an astute eye can immediately recognize when a student is out of balance [17,33] *as* shown in these three photographs 9, 23, and 34.
- ➤ The coach's highest priority is your child's safety. The ski instructor should always select a terrain steepness that matches his/her capabilities. The coach should be able to teach the different size wedges (Pizzas) and how they affect speed control. In addition, the ski instructor should inform your child how the different shaped

  turns can also affect speed *control.*[3, 5, 12, 16, 30, 33]

- ➤ When a child goes at speed that are beyond his/her control, they will tend to lose balance by leaning back because of the *fear* [16] *factor.* The instructor should have tools (Plastic hoops, ski harness, ski poles) available to assist your child to control his/her speed down the hill. To stay forward and be in balance, I play a game of placing a $100 (Play money) between the student's shin and the tongue of the boot. I'll tell the child that, "if they lean back on their heels, the $100 bill will fly out of the boot, and they will have to pay me back the money."

Figure 9. Losing the $100 bill because the student leaned back, causing the loss of shin contact from the tongue of the boot and being unbalanced.[15]

These are some **major challenges** that you may anticipate with this age group:

- Walking around in their heavy ski boots

- Maneuvering their heavy and cumbersome skis around on flat land.

- Achieving the correct athletic **stance6** (See photos 21, 22, 49).

- Making directional changes with different turn shapes.

- Learning how to stop.

- Learning how to get up after a fall (See photo 27).

- Climbing the hill (Side steps, herringbone, or "V" steps).

- Controlling the child's speed down the hill.[13,33] Coaches spend the majority of their time teaching effective and efficient turning with a variety of tools and drills. See figures 6-9 and photos 10, 11, 18, 19, 20-21, 26, 31, 33, 35, 36, 38, 40, 41, 46, 52.

bid you teach *speed control?*

(1   ) Did you select the proper terrain steepness?

(2   Did you teach the proper turn shape?

(3   What size wedge did the student use?

(4   How long did the child remain in the fall line?

(5   Did the student remain in balance throughout the turns?

(6   Did the child use wedge turn or parallel turns?

(7   How many turns did the student make, knowing that the more turns result in slower speed down the hill?

(8   *Are any* special ski tools being used to control the speed?

- Difficulty bonding with the coach.

Photo 29. *Group lessons can be fun and successful if structured properly. These kids had a blast and are coming back for their third lesson.*

- Constant crying due to separation anxiety from the parents. You may want to do magic tricks to create bonding and trust or just do snow angles.

What to expect for 7- to 10-year-old students

Before the lesson:

➤ This group of students should be able to do what the 3- to 6-year-old kids did but on a steeper grade hill and longer runs.

➤ The child may even be able to ride the conveyer belt or other forms of conveyor systems to transport people to the top or halfway up the beginner slope and work their way down making controlled linked C-Turns or J-turns.

Photo 30. *A four-year-old girl is being assisted by a ski instructor to load onto the people-mover conveyor system for safety.*

➢ The focus for this group should be on balancing and the three skills[33] (Edge-, pressure-, rotary-control) with longer and steeper runs on the beginner hill. The introduction of other movements (The Five-Fundamentals of Skiing Model[33]) should be part of this lesson.

➢ Balancing movements[33] are paramount in skiing. Scooting around on one ski making figure 8s and circles in both directions will help to reinforce balancing movements on one ski as the child scoots around on the snow (See photo 20). I should mention the majority of the time, you actually ski with most of your weight and balance on one ski.

- ➤ Like the previous age group, another balancing exercise is trying to stay balanced (Fore/aft, vertical, and lateral balance) is a great exercise. I will often tell the parents that they can build a low-beam exercise platform by using an 8' x 4" x 4" lumber and attach to each end a 4" x 4" X 4' lumber for stability. Whenever I have a gymnast as a student, they will excel in skiing at a faster rate because they excel in balance.

Photo 31. *A young gymnast on a balance beam practicing fore/aft, vertical and lateral balance.*

> If you're not interested in building a balancing beam, you can purchase a bongo board, balancing boards, or balancing balls. As coaches, we use many drills and ski tool[3, 5, 12, 13, 34]to practice balance and other skills.[3, 4, 23, 16, 26, 31, *33 33*]

During the Lesson

➢ The coach will cover more extensively on balancing and the three other skills33 (Edge-, pressure-, and rotary-control).

➢ The instructor will refine the Five Fundamental of Skiing Model.[33]

➢ The child should be taught the side-step (See photo 24) and herringbone steps (See photo 32) to climb up a steeper slope and even different snow textures (Soft, mushy, ice).

Photo 32. A timid 7-year-old girl learning to stay balanced on her skis as she progresses down a gentle hill.

As this group advances, they will be taught to load, ride, and unload on the conveyer-belt system to the top of the slope (See photos 40 and 41). If the run from the top of the hill is beyond their capabilities, we have an alternate means of going only partially up the hill by limiting the number of 2' x 2' carpet squares used. (See photo 33).

Photo 33. *2' x 2' carpet squares can be used to help children to meet their safety needs and skill level by adjusting the number of squares used to adjust the length up the slope.*

> ➢ More drills may be planned that focus on being balanced on the moving skis. Achieving a good athletic stance should be the goal because of the importance of good balance.[33] (See photographs 10, 11, 19-22, 35-38, 42-44, 46, 52).
> ➢ Other games the utilize skills (Edging-, pressure-, and rotarycontrol[33]) should be utilized to enhance the turning process.
> ➢ Wedge-changeups should be on the coach's menu. One of the common errors with wedge platforms is having too wide a wedge

Photo 34. *A young girl with too wide a wedge platform, which is causing her to sit back (COM falls behind the BOS*[6, 33]*) resulting the student to be out of balance.*

- ➢ Making J-turns[13, 33] and coming to a complete stop can be another task that should be taught (See figure 7).
- ➢ Making C-turns[13, 33] to slow down at the end of the turn is critical to be able to realign and rebalance before the next turn.
- ➢ One of my pet peeves is when a coach did not fully explain to the student *speed control. See* page 48 for a full explanation of *Speed Control.*
- ➢ Your child may be taught to ride the people mover carpet (Also called conveyer belt), to transport him/her to the top or halfway up the slope so they can safely work their way down the hill making linked-C turns.[13, 33]

After the ski lesson:

- ➢ Everything covered in the 3- to 4-year-old section should be covered her for this age group.
- ➢ Did the coach summarize what, where, how, and why you did those drills?
- ➢ Did you ask your coach if You or your child had any questions?

> Did the coach leave your child with any positive comments?
  The ski instructor should prime the parents on what to expect in the next lesson

These are the **major challenges** that you can expect for this age group:

- Achieving the proper athletic stance through the turns.[6, 33]

- *Fear*[16] *of* the steeper hills. The coach should teach how to conquer the fear by first going on less steep terrain and going down the hill slowly.

- Learning the Skill Concept Model[33] and blending it into the Five Fundamentals of Skiing Model.[33]

- Teach the many ways of controlling their speed down the slopes.[4, 23, 25, 30, 33]

For instance, completing the C-turns; going traverse across the slope; doing the J-turns.

- Continue bonding with the student.
- Adding more fun games, which teaches skills for proper skiing.

For the 11-year-old and older children:

Before the Lesson:

> This group of students should be able to do what the 7 - to 10-years-old children did, but from the top to bottom of the whole beginner hill.

- The goals for this group are to use more of the terrain with different degrees of steepness, and to introduce more drills to cover all of the skills that are necessary to make smooth, controlled wedge turns. Linking the wedge turns under different terrain conditions will offer challenges for this age group.

- The students should be informed that more ski tools may be introduced because the steeper terrain may be used and more types of turns may be used. The coach may want to use a ski harness to adjust the student's speed down the steeper hill for safety reasons to protect all age groups.

- That means learning how to load, ride, and unload from the chairlift safely. Some kids (Beyond the three- to six-year-old group) need assistance to slow down when skiing down the hill with a hula hoop or ski harness or even poles.

Photo 35. A child is being assisted down the beginner's hill by using a plastic hoop to help control her speed [6, 33] and to assist the student to maintain balance and to help with the turns.

Photo 36. A harness is being used by a four-year-old girl to slow her down as she weaves in and out of each ski cone that is simulating a race course.

Ski poles may be used in several ways as a tool to help slow a student of all ages down the hill slowly and safely.

Photo37. A child is being assisted down the slope with the help of the ski instructor's pole.

Photo 38. A ski coach is skiing backwards with his ski poles extended out horizontally so that his student can grab onto it for speed control and to assist with the turning.

All this being said, these are average expectations. It depends on the child's abilities, the coach's teaching skills, and the snow conditions. Skiing on Icey conditions, in soft show (Mash potatoes) or on chunky ice (Ice cookies) will hamper the learning process because of the difficulty of skiing on those conditions. Even adults will encounter difficulties under those conditions.

➢ This might include a *summary on* what your child did, why he/she did those drills, and how he/she did those drills with an overall critique on your child's performance on the skis.

➢ Your child might be given *homework* to prepare for the next lesson. For instance, being a crane, stork, or flamingo; by balancing on one leg and lifting the other. Or by making pizza or French fries with their bare feet on paper plates on a carpet wood floor, ceramic tile, and linoleum (With talc under the plates for easier movements).

During the Ski Lesson:

➢ The child should be able to do what the 7- to 10-year-old children can do but, from the top to bottom of the entire beginner hill with grades of steepness and snow texture.

➢ Your child should be able to make different types and shapes of turns. The use of different fun games should be introduced to train the student's body movements to achieve the desired response of the skis.

All ages of skiers may have the potential of advancing quickly to ride the conveyer belt or chair lifts to get higher up on the hill. All students should be taught to Load, Ride, and Unload safely from the chairlift. Because most of the chairlift's accidents occur during the loading and unloading process, and less often during the riding process, let's recapitulate the process of loading, riding, and unloading the chairlift:

1. Quickly move up to the first marker and observe the next chair coming around.

2. Quickly follow the chair to the second marker (Loading zone), and turn around (to observe the side with the armrest and to watch for oncoming chair, and observe the chair coming).

3. If you have ski poles, place them in the hand furthest away from the armrest. The one-hand should grab the poles midway up to lift the basket high off the ground.

4. When the chair hits the back of your legs, grab the armrest and sit down with your buttocks all the way back. If you're carrying a backpack, have it removed before hand and place it on your lap when you're sited.

5. Pull the safety bar down. If you cannot, have the lift operator assist you.

6. Once in the chair, sit still on your ride up. Do not play with your friends. It becomes particularly dangerous when the chair gets slippery because of the wetness or when ice accumulates.

7. Do not slam your skis together to get the accumulated snow off the skis because the skis may come off and cause an accident below.

8. Pull up the safety bar when you approach the unloading area. Land on the unloading zone in a parallel position. *A* wedge platform may interfere with your partner's skis and cause an accident. Let the chair push you forward off the ramp.

9. Quickly ski out of the area to prevent congestion with the oncoming patrons.

10. For some unknown reason, most of the accidents on the ride up, and occur with females rather than with males; and the injuries occur with the lower leg (Femur fracture) and with head concussions.

Photo: 39. A four-year-old girl is being assisted by a ski instructor to load onto the conveyer belt for safety reasons.

Photo 40. When the child's buttock is below the chair, assistance will be needed

To help the student onto the chairlift, especially when it moves at a high speed. The coach can always tell the lift operator to slow the chair down.

Photo 41. Two coaches are safely unloading a four-year-old girl off the chairlift for the first time and will assist with the steep off ramp.

After the Ski Lesson

- ➤ These are average expectations for each age group discussed. It depends on the child's athleticism, the coach's teaching skills, and
- ➤ the snow conditions. Skiing in icy conditions, in soft snow (Mash potatoes)., or chunky ice (i.e., Ice cookies) will hamper the learning process.
- ➤ Many times, I said, "might include" on the expectations sections foreach age group because not all ski instructors teach alike. I have written a book, "A Compressive Guide for Coaching Children to Ski." Hopefully, this will narrow the gap between a great teacher and a not-so-great teacher.

➢ In Chapter 6, I will give you pointers on how to select a top-notch ski instructor. This is not found in any book or manual that I'm aware of as of this date.

Some of the *Major Challenges* that this group may encounter are:

- Achieving the correct athletic stance[5] throughout all of the different types of ski turns and different shape ski turns.[3, 12, 33]

- Conquering fear when on a steeper hill.

- Can get bored easily or can't wait to show off to their friends or other people on the slopes.

- Not understanding the consequences of bombing the hill at Mache2 speeds.

- Making unnecessary foolish, risky stunts that compromise the safety of others and themselves. The wisdom and logic center resides in the frontal lobe of the brain. That center gets fully matured by the age of 25. With some adults, I wonder if their brain is fully matured the way they ski on the hill!

- The need to make further refinement of the Skiing Concept Model[33] to make the students more proficient using the Five Fundamentals of Skiing Mode.[33]

- While saved for a latter lesson, a child that is ahead of schedule because of their athleticism may get a coach to move ahead to refine the smoothness of the child's turns. The turns should be as smooth as hot butter rolling down a hot corn when going from turn to turn. If instead the turns are jerky and mechanical, the ski instructor may get the child to visualize and feel the lack of fluidity of the turns. When I see that lack of fluidity in their turns, I ask the student, "If he/she wants their friends to think that he/she is Rob/Robbie the Robot on the ski hill?"

Figure 11. Robotic movements are not fluid, but instead, it looks mechanical and jerky[16, 25, 33]

- I have emphasized repeatedly the importance of balance. What is critical is being balanced on both feet and balanced on one foot.

Photo 42. A three-year-old boy using a large steering wheel to remind him to keep his hands forward for better balance on both skis.

Photo 43. A four-year-old girl is executing a perfect left turn by utilizing all Five Fundamentals of Skiing.6, 33

- When children are taught correctly, you will see some amazing results. These children have building blocks established to build a castle.

Photo 44. A twelve-year-old boy is using the Five Fundamentals of Sking6, 33when making a left turn. Notice that he transfers his weight to the right ski and extends his right leg (long leg), which causes the right ski edge to engage into the snow with pressure, and by having the left ski flatten out by retracting the left leg (short leg).

Having a good athletic stance to achieve good balance throughout the turns is a mandate. Most skiers have not mastered the athletic stance. We coach them to "stand like an athlete", and we demonstrate the stance to them repeatedly, but they still don't get it. Let's try a different approach by emulating the stick model in front of the mirror.

Photo 45. *A* 12-year -old boy that is not balanced. He has most of his weight on the uphill skis instead of the downhill skis.

There are two exercises that a yoga instructor taught me to strengthen the ligaments and muscles of the ankles and to make them more flexible and pliable by pointing the toes down and all the way up for 15 minutes daily. The second exercise is to point the toes counter-clockwise direction and counterclockwise direction for 15 minutes daily.

- In Chapter 6, I will give you pointers on how to select a top-notch ski coach. This discussion is not found in any book or manual that I know as of this date.

CHAPTER 6

How to Choose the Best Coach for your Child

Countless parents have had the same experience of not liking the assigned ski instructor because they did not know any better. Selecting a top-notch ski coach for your child is a daunting experience. All parents are looking for value and for their child's success. You made the sacrifice to drive your child to the ski resort, made the investments on his/her ski outfit and equipment, and paid for the lift ticket and ski lesson. How do you know which coach is the best and which coach is just mediocre? Do you know what to expect from a coach?

In practice, when you go to the Snow Sports desk for a ski coach, they will assign one for you, based on the availability *of* the existing ski instructors. Some desks are good at this responsibility, some are not so good. So, what can you do? I will help prepare you with this important task. Here are my suggestions:

- ➢ You can ask the personnel at the desk for a PSIA Children's Specialist Coach; they are either certified as a Levels 1-3 (Being the highest) certified coach. A few might have PSIA Children's Trainer certification, to allow them to train ski instructors.

- ➢ Ask how many years has he/she been a children's coach? Generally, it takes a ski instructor over a decade to learn all of the tricks of the trade to become an accomplished coach.

- ➢ How good is the coach with bonding with kids and their parents?

- ➢ Does the instructor use a lot of props, tools, and games in his/her lesson?

- ➢ How funny is the coach? Does he/she use a lot of fun games to teach toe proper skiing movements?

- Has the coach been involved with any accidents with kids?
- Has there been any incidence with the coach not delivering the product or had any confrontations or complaints with the parent or the child?
- Did the coach look presentable, friendly, gentle, kind, and caring, fun-loving, which helps facilitate the bonding process?
- Do ask your child what gender coach they want. Boys are generally not fussy; girls can be.
- At the end of the lesson, you need to verify what the front desk told you about the coach's profile?
- Does the recommended ski instructor have a lot of returning clients?
- Is the coach's schedule filled most of the time? Is he/she always solidly booked throughout the week?
- Is the coach dependable and always tries to exceed *Customer Satisfaction?*
- How innovative is the coach?

Photo 46. Ski brushes are useful tools to teach different size turning as seen in this four-year-old girl doing small-radius turns at the top of the hill and large-radius turns at the bottom off the slope. In addition, balance is being continually worked on throughout the turns.

Photo 47. Because balance [6, 33]is so critical in skiing, two coaches from the Express Preschool Program are critically assessing a four-year-old boy with a plastic wheel in he is in a good athletic stance. [6,33]

- ➤ Has the coach achieved any accolades, such as Ski Instructor of the year, MVP coach for children, Best Teacher Award?
- ➤ If you did some initial scouting by asking friends about great coaches, gather your data for expedient success between instructor and parent at the scheduling desk.
- ➤ All else fails: ask the scheduling desk who are your top three kid's coaches?
- ➤ Once you find a coach, book in advance for the date and time you want.
- ➤ At the end of the lesson, verify what the scheduling desk told you was true.

- Did the coach have the personality, qualities, and skills of being an outstanding ski instructor?
- Did the coach look presentable, friendly, gentle, kind, caring, and fun-loving, which help facilitate the bonding process?
- At the end of the lesson, did the coach ask your child to tell you about what he/she learned in the lesson?
- Did the coach give positive feedback about your child's performance in the lesson?
- Did the instructor employ many fun games to teach skiing movements to get the ski to move as expected?
- Did the coach use ski tools to assist your child?
- Did your child learn the ABCs of safety?
- Most importantly, did the coach ask you, the parent, have any questions or comments to make?
- What score would you give the coach for Exceeding Customer Satisfaction21? Using a scoring system of 0 (not being great) to 10 (Outstanding) how would you evaluate the instructor?

Most of the time, you will succeed in finding an outstanding coach for your child. Like finding a great doctor or a great auto mechanic, it takes some time and research. Do ask around; ask your friends who have taken terrific lessons from a specific ski instructor.

Bonding is a very critical step when selecting a great coach. If your child has difficulty bonding with the instructor, it is a start to an uphill battle with a slower learning process for your child. Using a multitude of tools and props can greatly add to the success of the lesson. Let me share with two examples:

At the beginning of the ski season, I had a referral lesson from another parent who had a child take lessons from me. The student was a 5-year-old girl, named Savannah who never did any snow sports. She was just adorable and was, at first, shy and quiet. During my introduction, her mom said that Savannah was afraid of speed and heights. So, I took Savannah to a 3-foot runoff. This tiny munchkin was petrified to move. I immediately knew that I had to earn her **TRUST** through **BONDING.** I said to Savannah, *"I'm going to protect you as if you* were *my very own child, at all times."* I also stated that "we *will not go any higher on the hill until you say so, because you're the BOSS; I'll do want ever YOU want."*

I proceeded to attach a ski harness to her waist. After learning to make a Pizza, she went down the runoff very slowly as I regulated her speed with the harness, which gave her the confidence to try. She was having a blast, having fun with the different games we played, and she talked endlessly and was always smiling. We continued this activity for half-an-hour (Half the allotted time for the lesson). During that period, I assessed her profile: on a scale of 1-10 (with 10 being the

Best), her Cognitive development was 12, an Affective development of 10, and Physical development of 9.5. By the end of the lesson, she was able to do linked-wedge turns. I asked Savannah, "what *do you think about skiing?"* She said, "I never *had so much fun!"* Guess what? I was booked with her for the next five weeks. By the last lesson, Savannah progressed to being able to follow me down all the advanced slopes (Black Diamond), making beautiful, controlled parallel C-turns; AND I got invited to Anna's 6th birthday party with her friends that summer at their home. Now, that building **Bonding and Trust!**

Photo 48. A young girl is expressing extreme happiness and joy and one thumb's up because she followed her coach down an advanced slope (Black Diamond) making controlled, parallel C-turns all the way down to the bottom.

The second story is about Memory, a 3-year-old girl, who came for her first ski lesson. She and her dad were at the ski school front desk to book a lesson with me. I realized that she was afraid and did not want to go on the snow. There also appeared to be separation anxiety involved because she had her arms wrapped tightly around her dad's leg. She squeezed his leg tighter when he urged her to go and have fun. Soon she had tears. I told her that, *"I was Pineapple Herb and that I had magical powers to always keep her safe at all times and promised her to have tons of fun on the snow."* I did three different magical tricks. She was in awe. To my surprise, she took my hand and walked out to the snow without a whimper. I also asked her, *"if she would like Kermit the Frog to ride on her back as we skied?"* She said, *"yes!"* Boy, was she excited!

The purpose of using Kermit the Frog was to entertain her on the snow and, more importantly, to have her bend from the hips to achieve a slight angle (About 30 degrees) on her back to achieve an athletic stand for better balance on the skis. I told her that, *"if you stand upright, Kermit will slide down her back: but if she tilted her back a little, Kermit will be able to hang on for the ride."* I explained to the dad where we would meet after the lesson, and where he could watch our lesson unfold. We were hopping in the snow like crazy jackrabbits. We then lifted one foot up while balancing on the other foot, pretending that we were Flamingos. Next, we went sliding down the hill slowly (With a ski harness attached to her waist) with her feet making a Pizza of various sizes. I told Abby, *"I'm tired of pizza, let's make French fries and go down the little hill."*

In the end, I asked Memory, *"what did you think about your first ski lesson?* She said that, I asked her, "what do you think about your ski lesson?"

She said, "I want to come back to you.; I had so much fun! I didn't know that skiing was this exciting."

We walked in hand-in-hand into the lodge where I took my 12 pages of stickers and had her select one sticker. I always reward children with stickers for their efforts and successes.

While she was occupied, I discussed with her parents, what, why, how, and where we did our drills. I also asked Abby to tell her parents what she learned about safety.

She picked a Unicorn Horse and placed it on the front of her helmet. I was booked with Memory for the rest of the season.

The point of this story is an instructor must be creative, be able to analyze and fix children's anxieties, and provide fun games that will promote the proper body movements to get those skis to turn in control.

FUN[16] is the name of the game; having the kids do fun games without them knowing that they are actually learning movements with their bodies to get the skis to respond appropriately, is the mission of every good coach. We are in the **Entertainment Business.** Every coach should follow the **Unwritten Code** *on ensuring that every child has a happy smile at the end of a fun-filled lesson.*

Photo 49. A *coach is pretending to be a reindeer to entertain the children on the beginner hill.*

You can generally tell if the students are enjoying the ski instructor by their reaction on the slope—they don't want the lesson to end, regardless of what they are learning or how long the lesson they signed up for.

Photo 50. After a long afternoon of free skiing and with lessons, the children and their coaches are still smiling.

Photo 51. If I have time, I will have a snowball fight with the student to help bond and develop trust with the child. If they are wearing helmets and goggles, I will aim below the head area; if they are not, I will just let them pelt me with snowballs.

So, selecting A great coach is paramount to achieving rapid success with your child and exceeding customer satisfaction.21Based on your child's athleticism and quality of instructions that he/she receives, you will be thrilled with the rapid progress as shown in Photo 52, your child will acquire those same fundamentals of skiing and someday be a racer.

Photo 52. A preteen girl using the Five Fundamentals of skiing33to care turns around the slalom gates.

As a final reminder, I have emphasized safety throughout this book. *As* the child's performance level *increases,* the difficulty of the drills become more complex, the steepness *increases* on the terrain becomes more challenging, and as the speed increases, the danger also *increases.* The last thing that the coach wants is to report to the parents is that there has been a nasty accident (See figure 12). Be mindful that the coach's number one concern is your child's safety during the COVID-19 pandemic (See photo 53).

Figure 12. A young child in a nasty crash because she could not control the speed of her skiing.

Photo 53. During the COVID-19 pandemic, many new rules have been implemented at the ski resorts. Here you have a seven-year-old boy (wearing a face mask) with his private coach (who is wearing a double-face mask),

Be mindful, when you select the best coach, there is the potential of your child excelling in the lessons (See photo 54).

Photo 54. Mom and her 12-year-old daughter are jubilant because of the bonding and trust that they developed with the coach; In addition, they are thrilled with the rapid learning curve that their daughter made to be an advanced skier— whereby she has set her goal to be a ski instructor when she is of age.

In closing, as a parent, you now have the knowledge to better prepare your child for the first ski lesson.

WELCOME TO THE MAGICAL WORLD OF SKIING!

Photo 55. An exuberant little boy that made it to the top of the mountain and feeling that he is on top of the world!

REFERENCES

1. Adaptive Snowsports Instruction; PSIA Education Foundation, Lakewood, Colorado, 2003; 108 pages.

2. Anderson, John; Captain Zembo's Ski & Snowboarding Teaching
    Guide for Kids; PSIA Educational Foundation; Lakewood, Colorado, 2nd ed..; 1996; 33 pages.

3. Adult Alpine Teaching Handbook; PSIA-Vail and Beaver Creek Ski & Snowboard Schools; Beaver Creek, Colorado, 2011; 318 pages.

4. Alpine Handbook; PSIA Educational Foundation; Lakewood, Colorado, 1996; 77 pages.

5. Alpine & Snowboard Teaching Handbook, Vail Resorts Management Group; Vail, Colorado; 2004; 200 pages.

6. Alpine Technical Manual; PSIAA/AASI American Snowsports Education Foundation; 2014;150 pages.

7. Alpine Level I Study Guide; PSIA /AASI American Snowsports Education Foundation; Lakewood, Colorado, 1996; 126 pages.

8. Alpine Level II Study Guide; PSIA /AASI American Snowsports Education Foundation; Lakewood, Colorado, 1996; 95 pages.

9.   Alpine Level III Study Guide; PSIA /AASI American Snowsports Education Foundation; Lakewood, Colorado, 1996; 111 pages.

10.   Anderson, John; Captain Zembo's Ski & Snowboarding Teaching
Guide for Kids; PSIA Educational Foundation; Lakewood, Colorado, 2nd ed..; 1996; 33 pages.

11.   Brock smith, Dorfman, and Lichterman; How to Play Harmonica: A Complete Guide for Beginners; Adams Media, New York, New York, 1918; 175 pages.

12.   Children's Alpine Teaching Handbook; PSIA/AASI Intermountain (Northwest); 314 pages; 2010.

13.   Children's Instruction Manual, 2nd Edition; Product number 264; 2008; 128 pages.

14.   Cleeland, Mike and Everett, Alex; Ski Tips for Kids: Fun Instructional Techniques with Cartoons. ISBN: 978076270006; Falcon Guides; Guilford, Connecticut, 2013; 112 pages.

15.   Core Concepts for Snowsports Instructors: Teaching; PSIA/AASI Education Foundation; Lakewood, Colorado, 2008; 90 pages.

16.   Cues to Ineffective and Effective Teaching; American Snowsports Education Foundation; PSIA Education Foundation, Lakewood, Colorado; 2008; 12 pages.

17.   Elbee, Viviane; Teach your Giraffe to Ski; Albert Witman & Co.;Park Ridge, Illinois, 2018; 32 pages.

18. Hamilton, Ray J.; Squirrels on Skis; Random House Books; New York, New York, 2013; 32 pages.

19. Herrin, Nicholas; PSIA-AASI's Commitment to Snowsports Education Foundation: Is Outlined in Best Practices for Teaching During COVID-19; 32 degrees; American Snowsports Education Foundation; Lakewood, Colorado, Fall 2020; pages 45-47.

20. Jay, Joshua; Magic; The Complete Course; Workman Publishing Company; New York, New York, 2008; pages 368.

21. Kazanjian, Kirk; Exceeding Customer Expectation; Random House Publication; New York, New York, 2007; 256 pages.

22. Ludlow, Libby; A-B-Skis: An Alphabet Book About the Magical World of Skiing; ISBN-13 number 978-17332-1107, 2019; 32 pages.

23. Maslow, A; A Theory of Human Motivation; Psychological Review; 50:370-396 (1943).

24. New Snowsport Instructor Guide; PSIA/AASI Inter-Mountain (West); PSIA Education Foundation; Lakewood, Colorado, 2018; 27 pages.

25. Park and Pipe Instructor's Guide: Freestyle; PSIA/AASI American Snowsports Education Foundation; Lakewood, Colorado, 2005; 156 pages.

26. Pavia, Audrey; Horses for Dummies; John Wiley & Sons; Columbus Publishing Labs; Columbus, Ohio, 1999; 400 pages.

27. Pogue, David; Magic for Dummies; IDG Books Worldwide, Inc; New York, New York, 1998; 369 pages.

28. Rueda, Claudia; Bunny Slopes; Chronicle Books; Columbus, Ohio, 2016; 60 pages.

29. Snowboard Teaching Handbook; PSIA Educational Foundation; Lakewood, Colorado, 2015; 358 pages.

30. Stadel man, Paul, and Fife, Bruce; Ventriloquism Made Easy; Piccadilly Books, Ltd; Colorado Springs, Colorado, 2003; 108 pages.

31. Swift, Sally; Centered Riding; St. Martin's Press; New York, New York, 1985; 208 pages.

32. Teaching Snowsports Manual; American Snowsports Education Association, Inc, Lakewood, Colorado, 1918; 262 pages.

33. Vail and Beaver Creek Children's Alpine Teaching Handbook; Vail Resorts Management Company, Vail, Colorado, 2004; 200 pages.

34. Valar, Paul, and Johnson, Jimmy; Skiing: The Athletic Institute; Sterling Publishing Company, New York, New York, 1966; 93 pages.

35. Van Dusen, Chris; Learning to Ski with Mr. Magee; Columbus Publishing Labs; Columbus, Ohio, 2010; 93 pages.

36. Wahba, A. and Bridge well, L.; Maslow Reconsidered: A Review of Research on the Need of Hierarchy Theory;

Organizational Research and Human Performance; 15:212-240 (1976).

37.   Weston, Hannah, and Bedingfield, Rachel; Connecting Training: The Heart and Science of Positive Horse Training; Connection Training Ltd.; Elsevier Publishing; Cambridge, Massachusetts; 2019; 206 pages.

38.   2020 Ski Instructor Survival Guide; Deer Valley Ski Resort; Deer Valley, Utah, 2019; 206 pages.

39.   2020 American Diabetes Association Standards of Medical Care in Diabetes; American Medical Association, Muncie, Indiana, 2019; 206 pages.

US Review of Books

5.0 ★★★★★

How to Prepare for Your Child's First Ski Lesson

by Herbert K. Naito

book review by Carolyn Davis

" No stone will be left unturned; you will be fully prepared for your child's first ski lesson."

The author's unique offering is a comprehensive guide to preparing anyone from age three to eighteen to ski. In addition to the standard areas of preparation such as outfits, appropriate ski poles (adjustable ones are more expensive but may be more beneficial to a very young skier), instruction on positions regarding the skier's body and posture, and finding the right coach for the young person, Naito briefly describes the perspective of each age group, the importance of proper nutrition and hydration, and additional aspects of preparation that usually are not covered in traditional lessons. One example is the importance of the ski student going to the bathroom prior to the lesson.

Naito's book focuses on appropriate mental and physical preparation, not only for the young person's first lesson but also for the outdoors in general. Intriguingly, the age groupings that the author employs in the text differ from what is frequently encountered in other disciplines. For example, the book includes eleven to eighteen -year-olds in one group, which in other arenas are a large and diverse span in growth and development. It also defines the mindsets of children and teenagers in broad, brief ways. However, the categories regarding everything the reader may want to know about preparing to ski appear all -inclusive and are clearly defined. Those who take these chapters to heart will have an education in skiing that will facilitate safety, function, and fun. To paraphrase from the book's introduction, when you know how and what you want, and how to look for it, you get a better fit.